Copyright @2021 by Mr. Alien

All rights reserved. No part of this book may be reproduced in any form or by any electronic or mechanical means, including information storage and retrieval systems, without permission in writing from the publisher and the author. By reviewers, who may quote brief passages in a review.

This publication contains the opinions and ideas of its author. It is intended to provide helpful and informative material on the subjects addressed in the publication. The author and publisher specifically disclaim all responsibility for any liability, loss or risk, personal or otherwise, which is incurred as a consequence, directly or indirectly, of the use and application of any of the contents of this book.

WORKBOOK PRESS LLC
187 E Warm Springs Rd,
Suite B285, Las Vegas, NV 89119, USA

Website:	https://workbookpress.com/
Hotline:	1-888-818-4856
Email:	admin@workbookpress.com

Ordering Information:
Quantity sales. Special discounts are available on quantity purchases by corporations, associations, and others. For details, contact the publisher at the address above.

ISBN-13:	978-1-957618-62-3 (Paperback Version)
	978-1-957618-63-0 (Digital Version)

REV. DATE: 02.08.2022

TABLE OF CONTENTS

INTRODUCTION *12*

CHAPTER 1 .... *16*

CHAPTER 2 .... *24*

CHAPTER 3 .... *30*

CHAPTER 4 .... *37*

CHAPTER 5 .... *43*

CHAPTER 6 .... *49*

CHAPTER 7 .... *68*

CHAPTER 8 .... *76*

CHAPTER 9 .... *86*

CHAPTER 10 .... *92*

THE REAL GOD

YOU MUST THINK IN SPIRIT!

I've heard it said, Jesus is God ...and that's not all, these hypocrites will lie from hell to infinity.....

But I'd be done hearing bout anything when they tell me that God is a trinity!

The Devil has hypnotized the entire planet! Why not you? Do you believe this? This cut is deep, it will offend!

It is written:
"If the light within you is darkness, oh how great that darkness is"!
Implied:
If the thing you believe to be true is in fact false, you are in deep trouble.
Why...?
Because from this point onward all your beliefs will be predicated upon a lie; and all your constructs will be flawed; for you will attempt to justify everything based on what was initially false; therefore you will descend deeper and deeper into error and wrong doing.
"Inside your tin-can there be worms"!

This book is an attack upon the hypocrites, those who formulate the lies... those responsible for making our light darkness.

It is amazingly simplistic information:
Poetic; philosophical and at times
Satirical... employing techniques to criticize foolishness and to expose the techniques of corruption employed against individuals by using ridicule or exaggeration...
Yet at all times concerned with and speaking what is truthful!

Behold: The Real God
By
Mr. nobody

God requires a man to stand in the gap that he might not annihilate us all.

THE REAL GOD!
(Intro)

Chapter 1) Quest to find the real God!

Chapter 2) Is God your God?

Chapter 3) The God of our faith!

Chapter 4) Let the battle begin!

Chapter 5) Your father is the devil!

Chapter 6) Is Jesus God?

Chapter 7) Jesus confesses his origin.

Chapter 8) God is not a trinity!

Chapter 9) Holy spirit God deception!

Chapter 10) The pleasures of an eternal life.

Chapter 11) Conclusion

Preface

I confess that I've become tired, even bored; of all the rhetoric from these useless preachers, for they speak many words; make many promises, and although there is sound I'm hearing, still their words are meaningless and empty.
99.9% of preachers are using scripts from Satan.

They speak of many wonders, always saying God is about to do this or that; but they are liars, they know nothing, for they themselves are empty vessels only capable of making loud noises.

They claim God's powers of physical healing; by chance, have you ever come across anyone of these preachers/ healers who can replace missing limbs?
(No chance)! Yet these hypocrites pretend to resurrect the dead.

Many of these so-called Holy men boldly show their tattoos. (This is an act against God, no matter the justification they use; and a vanity belonging to the children of this world) and you know it!

Many wear cut jeans whilst preaching.
(A positive connection to the influence of this system, and flagrant disrespect to someone holy; a hole in jeans is not holy jeans).
But you still remain oblivious to all this. Why?
Every year they make you a new promise that this time next year you will be a millionaire, or something else as spectacular, and though it fails every year, still you believe the next foolishness.

*By your own choice, you consent to blindness.
You are hypnotised and accept it willingly.*

*There are some of you who wish only to hear wonderful words no matter what lies they contain. Tell me sweet little lies you say.
You!!!...Will find no joy in this reading.*

*It is now time to shine the light on these cockroaches!
God calls you into his light!*

*And so now Holy Father, I beg; for the glory of your name and the salvation of your people I request an audience....
I pray that you discipline me accordingly
... even put me to death if I intentionally misrepresent or blaspheme your holy name.*

*People, know this...I am not seeking your approval;
(So you might get offended)
In fact many of you shall now be left behind as we explain spiritual things to spiritual people.*

*I know I take my life into my hands when I propose to speak on his behalf. Perhaps I'm a fool, yet if I refuse to speak I too will be punished.
Criticism is natural as these words are not meant for all... for man will not receive from God without first surrendering his animal.*

Your first clue in knowing that what I'm about to show you is the truth is that all those whom you know to be liars and hypocrites have this false doctrine in-common.

"Why do you seek the living amongst the dead"?

How then do you suppose God is in agreement with you when you think as they do... in that you also carry the brand marks of known liars and hypocrites? You cannot cross over with this baggage you are carrying!
Either I speak truth; am deceived or am a devil!
You decide... your decision will help you see what lies within you; whether you are of the spirit!
Now we shall unmask the devil!
The one in you...... though you be in denial!

Your allegiance is now being called into question!

Intro

*I've heard it said Jesus is God ...and that's not all, these hypocrites will lie from hell to infinity.....
But I'd be done believing in anything when they tell me that God is a trinity!*

Ultimate blasphemy!!!

If you are a victim of this lie, you are also a victim of mass hypnosis. (Deeeep deception)

The entire planet has been hypnotized!
It gets deeper ……

Dare you say I didn't know; how often were you told? If this surprises you, then know for sure you are also a captive. Here lies the evidence!
Escape!
God is not a Trinitarian mystery, but is mysterious beyond belief; (Only in that he is beyond our comprehension) "no one knows him; neither can he be known by anyone, except the son reveals him".
Those words are not mine, but were spoken by his son who has revealed him.
All those making claims to speak with God as if at the end of their telephone lines are liars, hypocrites and devils.
In search of this God I have been stabbed all over with many pains. I am an outcast; afraid of the consequence of this knowledge (as I do not run with the crowd) and have even been afraid of his acceptance in my efforts to acquire his favour. Why…?
Well can you tell me, if there is anyone you know that got close to God without severe suffering?

You people have not been told the half of it.
I write to you now with fear and in trepidation.

I fear God and do not wish to wrong him!

Father!!! Lord God of heaven and earth;
I.. need.. you! I.. need.. you! I.. NEED.. YOU!
Oh how I need you!
I beg of you dear God; pleassseee help me!

Why is it deemed necessary for you to hide?
You know we seek you!
Why should I assume these people will believe anything I say if you allow this blindness?
Please reveal yourself!!!

A response comes as a feeling that I can only assumed to be of God if these words are correct; it speaks in this way: "To you it is granted to know and to understand; but to these people it is not granted,

I am not the one they seek"!

I know a man, who was once invited into heaven, into the very presence of God, where he was shown a representation of God and of our lord Jesus; and was also allowed to speak in his presence before Angels.

I now offer you this insight. (I do appreciate the fact that because so many liars have preceded me, my words and information will appear false) However what I say, I say with all sincerity and in the fear of my own life. Please believe me!

The heart of the wicked one will have already prejudged me, so be it! Should I be concerned by the wicked? I think not! But if your heart is of God you will judge with righteous judgement. Your spirit will hear; and you will know if I speak truths, for it is the few to whom this message is intended. Therefore as it is written; let him who is of the spirit, hear what God says to his church.

So drastic are the changes that are now required, that only the few can make room for this spirit.
(Though many are called)
Do not think because you say: I believe there is one God that - that will suffice.
It is not enough for you to say I believe there is one God and this is why! James 2:19

Now the time has come to transcend denominational attachments and co-operate together to intensify the spirit warfare against demonic forces in high and low places.
(It is against demons we fight)

Also since scriptures confirm we ought not to say we follow Paul or Apollo; likewise we should not say we belong to any church but only to God.
Please note well this saying; any expression contrary to the word of God is from a demon.

CHAPTER 1
QUEST TO FIND THE REAL GOD

The one above all!

I've heard of a beetle that's a broach; I know of a cock that is a roach; but these preachers really takes the biscuit... they've lost their fear; they no longer care; they know they're lying and they don't intend to fix it.

People;... Of this one thing be assured!

Any preacher who speaks in tongues to the public is a devil. He does not speak to you and I, for we do not understand him. (He's crazy)
His words are not to God, for God has told him not to do this. (He's a rebel)
The inescapable conclusion therefore is ... this one is in conversation with the devil!
In this do you rejoice; how are you this blind?
You are in a den with demons!
(And so now you know)

These well known preachers (99.9%) of them literally stink of hypocrisy; (you know they're snakes, still you let them bite you). What prevents you adding 2+2 together? (Simple arithmetic's)...
You are under a spell!

Now look here...do not suppose that because your preacher has a private jet or has accumulated riches that he has found the way or has come in contact with God.

Neither should you believe that because he can tell you what you had for breakfast, that God is with him.

The foolishness people accept as proof of God belongs to dead people; there is no Holy spirit in the sayings of these men but you believe because it is what you want to hear; (Your desire for pleasure is overwhelming it is your delusion; that by which you are being deceived; and God has said he will send you this delusion) you do not want the truth; you remain unconcerned as to whether God is truly the source.

Neither should you suppose that because that one is eloquent in speech or handsome in appearance that God is with him!
This is the mentality of a child.

You know these ones are liars and hypocrites, yet you believe as they do. What are you?

If then he/she has a demon; so do you!
If they are wicked and sadistic; so are you!

You are seeing your reflection in the mirror!

So then where should we look for God?

God is not with the cream on the top, but he is with the hurting on the bottom. Not found amongst the mighty, but lives amongst the poor.

Now where am I going with this? I'm asking you, where are you looking for God now? Is he present because your church is big or your pastor is rich and mighty?

I could go on to talk about many other scenarios such as finding God in the wilderness with John the Baptist; or locating him in a food troths in a barn where lowly animals feed in the case of Jesus Christ.

But just in case you are irritated, stubborn or still blinded; finding this too hard to stomach because you refuse to learn from your mistakes or let go of your love for your pastor; who taught you not to own up to anything; may I ask you; please tell me how you reason with this?

Isaiah 57:15 **For this is what the high and lofty one says; he who inhabits eternity, whose name is holy. I live in that high and holy place with those whose spirit are contrite (those feeling sorry, apologetic,) and lowly to revive them.*

So now that God has told you where he lives (With humble lowly people) is this where you are looking? Will you accept him at his word or are you still determined to stick with your plan?

I beg of you oh God; please strengthen also my own Spirit and my resolve, (This is a difficult task and I too am hurting) for you know how hard it is to speak truth to these people!

So now onward to the task...; who is God and what does he want?
Why is it so hard and complicated to know and be obedient to his requirements?

Eve rejected him, Adam rejected him, Satan rejected him, one third of his Angels rejected him, and now most of mankind rejects him.

Moses accepted him and asked to be put to death.
Elijah accepted him and asked to be put to death.
Job cursed the day he was born.
Jeremiah cursed the day he was born;
(Because of hardships God made them suffer)
David chose to offend him and
Solomon abandoned him.
Now I ask you: what kind of résumé is this for a God that

requires my worship?

Anyone who enters into his presence is pressured and altered in the atmosphere.

Those who are saying, the real God gives you riches and prosperity, are liars and devils!
In the face of all this, is there still room for God in your life and in mine?

Let us unlock the path together if you want clarity and the ability to fix this relationship!
See if I speak the truth. Put these words to the test; or keep your satanic lifestyles! Yours to gamble with; though you know the devil is your owner.

Note well; we must be willing to surrender what we believe to be ours; even our very lives.

The human in us all must be broken!

Shadrach; Meshach and Abednego met God in the fire!
Daniel met God in the lions den; this is where he waits for you. This is our lowly place; the place where our words are proven true.
Our broken place where we all must surrender to our beliefs! These are not simply stories; neither can you avoid the consequences of being broken.
(You already are)!
The healthy does not need a physician.
The rich do not need God. What about you?

He doesn't answer when you call does he?
So why should you believe?

Did you approach God because you want to do right, or simply because you've harmed yourself?
Is it all because you hurt or because you care about the hurting? What you expect of God; is this also what you practice?
If you do right and help does not come you will have your day in court.
Justice demands it!

"If I speak wrongly bear witness concerning the wrong, but if rightly why would you hit me"?

Luke 4:18-19

The spirit of the Lord is upon me, because he has anointed me to preach the good news to the poor. He has sent me to heal the broken hearted, to preach deliverance to the captives, and the recovering of sight for the blind, to release the oppressed, and to proclaim that the Lords favour has come.

However, there are those whom God cannot reach.
Has he not told you?
All those who receive Intel from the intelligent!

Do you suppose we could live our lives on our merits and stand before God by our wisdom, cunning, and human intelligence as approved?

What really do you think God amounts to that he can be reached by our efforts?
How can he be God if our intelligence is a match for his?

If we are refusing to break the human in us, how will the God in us come forth?

Matthew 16:23/25
Whoever wants to save his life shall lose it; but whoever loses his life on my account will gain it.
Are his words of any help to you?

John 21:15-17

Simon; do you love me more than these?
Then feed my sheep!
(Let go of what you want... do what I ask)

Earlier for fear of death Peter lied, and said he did not know Jesus.
Now he has returned to his old lifestyle.
Jesus pushes Peter to always look to the life he has chosen and the love he professes for him;
by asking three times, this will hurt and shame him.
This pain he will remember for the cut is deep; and it will always be there as his reason for being a Christian.

Now you too are being challenged and changed.
Do you work for this life or the one to come?
How deep is your cut; will you obey?

It's gonna hurt some more!

This is not for all; God knows who are his.
"These people honour me only with their mouths, but their hearts are far from me".

Will the pastor surrender his private jet?
I think not!
(Although the private jet is not the sin)

Mark 10:17-30
One thing is missing... you are rich, your dependency is on money and not God; give it to the poor!
Was the rich man compliant?
You must be having a laugh...; for a rich man to surrender his riches, you must put a gun to his head!
(Even then he will not; although there is the exception)
However, is it still your claim that Jesus encourages riches?

It is really a difficult thing for the rich to enter heaven. Even though this hurts, you know it is the truth. Why then increase your handicap!

Luke 19:8-10
Now judge for yourself!

CHAPTER 2

IS GOD YOUR GOD?

In beauty; he is indescribable...
In wisdom; he is beyond questions...
In personality; he is flawless...
In power; majestic...
In love; matchless; there is no other like him.
There can only be one!

If your belief is that God is a trinity; this is not your God.
The Trinitarian doctrine is blasphemy!

You know that he is not your God by your inability to repent...you belong to another.

People the time is coming; it is in fact now here; your time of decision. God will make himself known to the blessings of some and to the detriment of others.
This God; who in the beginning made the heavens and the earth, the being who brought all things into existence, has now brought himself into controversy and contention with all mankind.
He requires answers from us for our recalcitrant behaviour. A reason for our stubborn denials; therefore prepare your defence!

"How can I know without some one to teach; and how can he teach without being sent"?

In this saying God lays the responsibility upon himself to provide truths.
(His words are backed by his spirit; thus proof of spirit is therefore required)

Immediately we can omit all books which are not within the grasps of all; meaning also all the books of the apocrypha as it is outside the reach of common folk and difficult for some to obtain. We use the books from which Jesus and his apostles quote.

Simple common sense says if God will save you he must show the way. Yet there are many preachers with frogs in their mouths, (Lying spirits) having information they claim to be from God which cannot be verified; demonic pastors put in high places to deceive.

The church of Satan gained acceptance to worship in the u.s.a in 1966.
The sorcerer gave a hand sign, a symbolic gesture to demonstrate how he evokes Satan.
I behold endless pastors using this same gesture throughout their worship with you in attendance.
I tell you;
You do not know God but you do know the devil!

These are your pastors of whom I speak.

It is written: Test the spirit!
In this way you will know if your beliefs are similar.

But this I am sure you know; no one who speaks by Holy Spirit contradicts the word of God.

It is implied in scripture that there were some 450 false prophets to every true servant of God....can you possibly calculate the odds today?
Have you been asleep all this time?

There are many hypocritical liars out there who fish for us with baits designed to ensnare us; because we are selfish; we are insincere, lustful and greedy lukewarm Christians, we desire an easy life.

In other words we want a piece of God but are unwilling to accept the part that corrects us or makes us uncomfortable.

You are not really looking for God;

*You wish to make God conform. Where God disagrees you will side step his words.
(As you are doing now)*

*Well excuse.... me, but you are an easy target, primed for wickedness; because there is always someone who will pay the price you require.
For many will not accept warnings, until the situation is upon them; having thus far avoided the consequences of their sins.
(Not punished for their many unfaithful acts, or their lies; escaped prison for things they've done, and even avoided many diseases etc) Yet even though confused and conflicted, they refuse to entertain any thoughts other than their own.
(Wat a ting !!!) Madness!... C'est la vie!*

Which false prophet was used to ensnare you? What tricks did this devil use, was it your pride; your intelligence; did you simply want money, or did you just fall from some other great height. In either case you are still falling, no matter how your life appears.

The real question now requiring your answer is:
Whom do you believe you have been introduced to; do you still believe your God is God?
Is he also for sale?

Does your hypocrisy stretch so far that you allow yourself to believe your half hearted attempts at righteousness gains you his approval? (Confess)!!!

You know your god is not God!

How can he be since your beliefs fall within the parameters of these serpentine satanic prophets?

Isaiah 6:9-10

.... *hear again and again, but do not understand; see again and again but never get knowledge; make the heart of this people unreceptive, and make their ears unresponsive, and paste their eyes together that they may not see...... that they may not actually turn back and get healing.*

Why does God speak this way?
Because he had encountered an unyielding stubborn and stiffed necked people!

What is your reason for believing you are different?
For you are saying to yourself, surely this is not referring to me!
Yet you are not any longer open to his word or to reasonableness!

You set your own standards, using words and expletives that cannot be found in scripture, but only by your intelligent deductions.

How can you pretend to align yourselves with God, and still be in competition with him?
How many fools have you murdered; persuading them to align them selves with you?
I ask you to please consider that you may be in the wrong even as I also must.
I can only pray that God will not need to express his anger on us both!
Are you in need of still more convincing?

Do you mean to say that there is nothing that has been said thus far that has moved you to reconsider or has been of any help to you... are you still not convinced?
If you keep it within your spirit that I am an idiot you will be able to hold onto your beliefs a little longer.

CHAPTER 3

THE GOD OF OUR FAITH

O God, I have faith in you, please help me where I'm lacking!

By way of testing our faith; Jesus says: He that is faithful in what is little is also faithful in what is much.

Translation by way of illustration:
Do not jump off a building and assume you can fly.
First jump from a chair, you will only break your ankle instead of loosing your life.

This is the point: If he (God) has not established your faith in the little things, do not move on to bigger and greater things; you will loose your life by your assumptions.

So then (See me!!!???); I do not wish publicly to assume to speak for God when he has told me nothing, and so I jump only from this tiny chair; the building is far too high... and I'm not a fool.

I have listened to so many ridiculously stupid things said in the name of God... The mind boggles in that you cannot see through the lies.
Empty demonic prophets that congregate on T/V chat shows saying enormously stupid things; whilst you the audience give your applause!

EG: In his visit to heaven he was eating pizza; or whilst in heaven rooms were observed that had body parts to replace ours. (Sacrilege)!
I hope there is a room also with heads to replace yours!

Jeremiah 15:1-2
The nonsense you people tolerate is truly incredible and then you wonder why he will not tolerate you!

So now should I jump because these fools do it?

Moving on: ....
Scriptures speak of the fruitage of the spirit.
Your production is evidence of your alignment.
The side you are on is shown in your behaviour.
EG: Can God be your God if you are a liar?

Has he made himself known; has he introduced himself to you? At some level he has already done so, that is his job (Even now I know he is still trying) but can you even hear, or are you now set in stone; being unmovable?

Perhaps you have a convenient God... Think!!!
What's that word they all use:

.........."unconditional" ......!!!

(Aha, that must be it, for it implies a God who loves you no matter what you do; a God who tolerates any and all of our idiotic behaviours).

Does your God have this "unconditional" love?
Foolish people;... you who allow yourselves to be deceived and brainwashed because you do not want to change.
You insist that God should love you the way you are. Why then is there a Devil? Does God love the devil the way he is?
Stubborn foolish people! If this is your belief, you should know you are actually children of the Devil, for you think as he does.
Have you not seen the destruction God has brought upon soooo many to show his conditions must be met?
How can God hate and still have unconditional love?
What nonsense!!!!!
For God sake as well as your own, use common sense; what

was the purpose of the 10 commandments?

If you are concerned about life, then it is time you make sure; put your belief to the test.
The judgement for error is arriving; and you are in the way; though you act without care, your actions shall not be without consequence.
You shall know this soon enough.
(As did five foolish virgins)

Test what you've been told against what is written.

(Man vs God).

We all already have a god of our own bias; based on our personal beliefs, and our shameful conduct, and to add to our shame, based also on the ideas and thoughts of foolish men.
We make men gods, when we accept their knowledge above what has been presented as God's written word.

You are no different from an evolutionist; you merely have added the "god" element, but then have reverted to type?

If you believe in evolution, whose idea is that? It certainly was not yours; maybe you accept science; are you a scientist?
So then, in what god do you believe?
The originator of the words you now believe is your god.
(Same for all your other beliefs... you are not the first in it, so who do you worship)?
When they change their minds, (as men often do) then you are left in your foolishness attempting to justify it.
Does it please you to live in another man's toilet?

Do you simply regurgitate the foolishness of others?

*I am a simple child. I hope I am also God fearing.
If I do not see words like "Elohim" and "Yeshua" in my
scriptures, (Not stating error) I am inclined to abstain.
I will not be brainwashed by intellectuals. "Man must live
not on bread alone, but on every word that comes from the
mouth of God"!*

*Unconditional love is what we must have for God; not
him for us. He is not false and does not change, but we
are false, and are constantly changing. There is no such
scriptural obligation that binds God. You are once again
deceived!*

Satan's witches or his bitches, which?

*Lying and killing for your wicked pleasures or merely
surrendering to sexual desires; being creatures consumed
with lust.
Dogs in heat or ravenous wolves seeking gratification,
or are you merely his beasts of burden, a lover of wrong
doing!
Who are you? ... What are you?*

*You are under a spell; is it not yet apparent?
Doesn't matter, you will not be able to free yourselves!*

*If only you would confront your beliefs; spend some time in
face to face companion ship with your false gods;
(Get the atheist in a room with an Ouija board for a month)
then perhaps they could come to terms with their hypnosis;
with the knowledge that there's a giant hole in their heads.
A void; an empty place; words without substance;*

everlasting foolishness!

By the way... you are not obligated to accept God, so you need not accept anything; merely enjoy your temporary lives.

I am writing with urgency because it would seem to appear that the signs which we are observing seem to indicate your time of ignorance is almost up.

Those who decline to take the tests already show their guilt, in that they are not seeking truths.
However, since they do not believe what is it that they fear?

That we are so easily fooled by these people is often based on our own disposition in that we accept only what we want to accept and not because of a truth; either greed or selfishness will makes us easy prey.

You may choose to believe in nothing.
The fact that you choose not to put your thinking to good use also shows contempt for life. And so in this also you create your own God.
(There is no hiding place).

Others search not for God, but how to use the belief of God to prosper and make money.
They lie; scheme and murder to achieve the glory of this their true god (money); and kill in order to protect him.

Money maybe a powerful god, but its real value is only with the dying and the dead.

The true God is everlasting and eternal. All other attempts at god no matter how benign, magnificent or innocent they may appear; are constituted as worship of the devil.

As stated: *If your god is not the real God he is the devil! No hiding place for ignorance!*

So then, the challenge is:
Can you produce evidence that your God is the real one?

Do your arguments defend God, or do they defend the God you believe?
Can you find the difference between the two?

Proverbs 27:11

"Bless me heavenly father that I may make your heart rejoice and give to you a response for him who taunts you"!

You are my God! May my praise of you be true!

People; it is far more difficult to unlearn a thing than to learn it, as we look into our souls we encounter obstacles obstruction and pain.

We now must put our knowledge under the spotlight...
God help us!

Perhaps I'm still an idiot in your eyes; but I will keep making attempts to bring reasonable evidence to the table.

CHAPTER 4

LET THE BATTLE BEGIN..!

What was I fighting for… my god, how could I have been this blind?

Matthew 5:46-47//44-45// 48
(In this order)
If we love only those who love us what great thing are we doing, even wicked people do the same. Loving someone who is good to you is not love; you are merely being reciprocal or thankful; looking after your own interest. One may even say; you are simply selfish! How can you deny It? Are you able to love someone who hates you? This is the power of love which God demonstrates!

We must move away from our selfish love, our place of comfort; love isn't real until it hurts.

In this regard, God often goes missing in our lives that we may prove we love him just because.

2Chronicles 32:31

"So God left him alone to put him to the test to get to know what is in his heart"!

*Since God already knew? Then why test him?
And so by this inference, we see God will allow us to suffer; we must prove we love him because it is the right thing to do and not because of how it makes us feel or because there is dinner on the table. The results are immaterial.*

*Many times in tears I've pleaded: God I beg you, please, don't do me like this!
In the end just like our Lord Jesus I conceded.....
God; let your will be done!*

God is at war with us, he fights for our love.

God will break your heart!

*Why...? Because it has to be re-fashioned in his image, as presently it is not!
Don't pretend as though you don't know what I'm talking about! How often are you in tears? Is it for God or is it your own sorrows?
We shall not be granted many of our requests, for he will not give us a scorpion when it's an egg we need; neither are we given a snake in the place of a fish.*

Fools sing songs; "God has never failed me yet"; ... they lie, and lead us into false hope. Although God blesses he allows us to learn by failure.

Romans 8:20

It is written: "…creation was subject to futility, not by its own will, but by him who subjected it on the basis of hope".

I tell you a secret:
Do not be overly annoyed or angry at him/her who breaks your heart., Use it to cry out to God… he is calling you!
A broken heart is a necessity; he binds the broken heart; let God heal you; we must go to the brink and come back.
(Surrender)!

If our hearts are not broken how will we understand what it means to forgive?
It must be broken that we may abandon idolatry; and it is broken that we may be separated from Adam as our father.

We are broken that we may be made anew; that we may be re-assembled in the image of God.
(Via his son Jesus)
(This is what the father does with those he loves)

Hence God explains:
"You must be perfect as your heavenly father is perfect".

So now, let us attempt to place a revelation upon the statement concerning the love of God.

Toxic love carries bitterness, un-forgiveness, worry and pride; it produces anxiety, frustration loneliness and greed.

*The love of God carries the meaning of
"do no harm"!*

ICorinthians 13:4-8
Because of this it is understandable why some may think it is unconditional; (It is not) but evil will attempt to exploit good intent.

Take as an example Cain; who despite his own evil makes an appeal to God.
"You sentence me for killing and at the same time give permission for me to be killed"!
God's response implied: whosoever attempts to harm you will not go unpunished but will suffer seven times as much.

Genesis 4:13-15
Now I ask you; on what basis was Cain making his appeal? He is a murderer is he not?
Then shut your mouth and accept your punishment.

Not so with God; even with the wicked, justice is balanced; they are given rights.

Satan and his devils also seek to exploits this love.

Luke 8:28-33
"I beg you, do not torment me"... also they kept entreating him not to order them to go into the abyss.

Again I ask you, on what grounds or on what basis do such evil demons make an appeal?
To request mercy, begging that they themselves not be harmed!

Yet acting without mercy causing harm of the worst kind, tormenting and killing others; and then asking permission to escape it; incredible!
They seek to exploit God.
(As do you..... you who believe his love is unconditional....
You are being influenced and seduced by demons)

You are successful though you are corrupt and cruel, this is temporary; you cannot escape the reckoning to come.

Almost all examples I can presently think of comes under this category, even until now, wicked men and demons seek to exploit God's kindness.

Praying and begging God for mercy, whilst making a pretence at going to church but in fact are doing much harm to others.

Jeremiah 7:8-10/16

See! you are trusting in foolish words that cannot profit you. Do you really think you can steal, murder, commit adultery, speak lies, worship Baal and all other false gods, (Do as you please) then come here and stand before me in my house and believe you will be saved? Is my house like a den of robbers in your eyes? Do not pray to me on behalf of such people, (Do not beg me) neither try to make intercession to me on their behalf for I will not listen to you.

Behold! The unconditional love of fools; are you exempt; will you escape such foolishness?

It is not in the way or the love of God to harm another or cause to be harmed anyone whom he has created like himself.
Surely you know that God must have love for his own person!
Yet because there is justice in love, (balance and fairness) the one causing harm will himself be harmed that love may continue.
(This is simply a law of dynamics).
No escape here!

God is benevolent and kind.
This is the meaning of his loving grace;...
it refers to "kindness of the spirit".

"Grace" means undeserved kindness of the spirit.

"God be gracious to me a sinner"; is meant as God show me kindness despite myself.
However there will always be someone willing to take advantage of this kindness, because the devil is in our flesh.

Do you still find me unreasonable?

CHAPTER 5

YOUR FATHER IS THE DEVIL!

And so now you know it!

Is the Devil stupid?
You'd better believe it, yes he is; he is also a madman a monster and the ultimate predator; ...and so are all of you who thinks as he does.
What idiot can challenge God and say that he is in his right mind?
(Must you also contradict him?)

John 8:43-45

Why is it you do not understand what I 'm saying? It is because you cannot hear my words. You are from your father the devil, and you wish to carry out his desires. He was a murderer from the beginning; he cannot hear truth because there is no truth in him. When he speaks the lie he speaks according to his own disposition, because he is a liar and father to the lie. But I on the other hand tell you the truth and you do not believe me because you cannot....
(It is not in your D.N.A).

Demons imitate their master Satan,
(You must imitate yours) and so this is why you cannot believe; and why you cannot accept these words.

The only true God, the real God of heaven;
he is not your father.
He is not the one you serve.

Now enters the dragon to challenge and put God to the test. The original serpent/dragon; the first demon; god of all lies, your master and the one with whom you are agreement!

Job 1:6-12

That Satan is a senseless idiot; also a madman; and stupid beyond belief is a foregone conclusion.
Yet how does one account for the fact that he gets a third of the Angels to follow him, and that he has you confused unable to know the right thing to do?

God offers the man Job as one obedient.
"A man blameless, who turns aside from this foolishness and from wickedness"!

Satan's retort implies: You have empowered him, we are not fools; if you give free stuff anyone would follow you... but it means nothing!
Let him experience difficulty; make him join the struggle of life!
If I speak falsely then remove your hand that it may be proven, that all may see whether he will choose the path I offer or not!
I assure you he will curse you to your face!

Satan believes once pain or affliction takes hold, man's selfish nature kicks in and the devil in him (The Satan) will be revealed.
He intends to prove Job is more like him than God. That Job also is a devil at heart and is actually in chains.

God acquiesce; but with restrictions.

Satan does not succeed;... Job accepts his pain, and in his tears he concludes that God has this right to add or remove what is his as he sees fit.

However on another occasion in the assembly of the Angels, God brings up the fact that Satan has failed.

Satan's retort is that it was God's restrictions (not to touch Job himself) that has not allowed for a true test. Again God consents that Job may be harmed but not killed. (As that would prove nothing)

Job 2:3-6 Again Satan fails.
What is it that helps us reveal the real God?
He does not require his people to harm or be harmed.
God said: He is still holding firmly to his integrity even though you try to incite me against him to swallow him up; to harm him without cause.
The tremendous efforts made by God to save man cannot be overlooked!
The devil has allowed us to see the depths of God's love.

What is the greatest test of love?
John 15:13
"No one has love greater than this, that one should surrender his soul in behalf of his friend".
If we truly wish no harm to another, we will do all we can to save their lives; which helps to explain why rich people seldom qualify.
The resource that keeps them rich are resources they covet to the detriment of others.

In his separation of the sheep from the goats Jesus says at Matt 25:35-40:

"I became hungry and you gave me food.... Thirsty and you gave me water..... A stranger and you received me hospitably... naked and you clothed me... sick and you looked after me... in prison and you visited me.
The sheep (righteous ones) replied "lord when did we do these things"?
Jesus replies "truly to the extent that you did this to one of the least of these my brothers, you did it also to me".

I say to you people; do no harm to one another, help your brother, for that one stands in the place of Jesus Christ!

JOHN 3:16

"For God so loved the world that he gave his only begotten son"
He did it first... He teaches by example.
He allows harm to come to himself (Via Jesus) that we might understand his love.
Jesus stands between us and the enemy to make God understood. When we understand we shall also do the same for our brethren.
Herein lies my attempt to pass on these lesson in love.

But since Satan persecuted Jesus, he will persecute us also!

2Corinthians 11:13-15

For such men are false apostles, deceitful workers, transforming themselves into Apostles of Christ and this is no marvel for even Satan (Disguises) transform himself into an angel of light; so then, it is not a strange thing that his servants (Disguises) transforms themselves into teachers of righteousness. But know this; their end is assured.

We therefore prove to be children of God by the love we show each other.
I say to you however, if your thoughts are in anyway similar to that suggested by Satan, then he is your father; can you still be in any doubt?

And I tell you still further;... whenever you desire to side step God's word for your preference you are the devil's child.

*And here is another test:
God disapproved of Jobs 3 comforters; in that they were agents of the devil. Are you?
If you are unable to spot their deceitful rhetoric then it is likely Satan is also using the same tactics on you.*

It matters not if you accept these words as truth, for if you still remain blind it is because this is how you like it!

The graves are filled with his conquests for your father the devil is a natural born killer!

God on the other hand; does not wish to harm anyone!

*Ezekiel 18:23
Do I take any delight at all in the death of someone wicked?*

Incidentally this is a good scripture to note for a discussion in my other book which revolves around the topic of hell-fire!

CHAPTER 6

IS JESUS GOD?

O Jesus, God of all that is, why do you not answer me? I implore you, help me; what is it you want of me what is my sin Lord? Nonsense!!!

These word maybe the words you pray. It is well intended; yet it is based on a lack of knowledge!!!

You say Jesus is God, and yet he alone is not God for he needs the father and the Spirit to fulfil him; tell me how can Jesus being God need anything at all or depend on your logic to maintain him"?

How Satan must laugh at your stubbornness?
In you he has found another rebel.
How long will God put up with your foolishness?

Thou art my son, this day I have begotten thee!
God has spoken!

God (Jehovah) says of Jesus: He is my son.
Jesus says of God: He is my father, I am his son.
The bible narrators say: He is Gods son.
Evil demons say: You are Gods son.
Satan the devil says: If you are God's son; prove it!
But you say.... Jesus is not simply Gods son;
Jesus is God!
Wow!!!... What rebels you are!

The front you people have that you can propose a lie of such magnitude that even the devil envies you; and all this you do in the face of such overwhelming evidence.
It is unconscionable that a human being should be this wicked.
Can you imagine this, that you can be termed a devil, with greater designs on wickedness and deception than the original liar?
(Do you now see why he has recruited you?)
The devil asked for proof of son ship, but you contradict everything and make even stronger assertions than he does.

*Matthew 16:13-17 Who do men say that the son of man is...
And who do you say I am?
The world is not expected to accept this answer, but you should accept it, for it is expected of those who claim to know God.
(Stop your blasphemy)!
Why can you not accept that Jesus is the son of man from his own mouth, and the answer that he is son of God from Peter's mouth?
(Ordained by God)
For Jesus said: You would not have known this except my father revealed it to you. This is why you cannot accept it, you are not his children.
God told Peter, Jesus is my son. You cannot say Jesus is God without contradicting this!
Cease your blasphemy, you demon!!!*

You are simply a tool being used by Satan because of your pride. You claim to believe it and then with your next breath you contradict it and say Jesus is God!

*As a form of reference; if asked what is God to you, would you not say... he is my father?
This can only be true of righteous ones, deemed perfect in God's eyes.
Did not Jesus also say he is my father?
Jesus also says: I am your brother... Do you oh foolish man, claim to be the brother of God?*

*ITimothy 2:5
How pray tell; do you explain this?*

"For there is one God and one mediator between

God and men; the man Christ Jesus"!

Is God the mediator... No!
Is Jesus Christ the mediator.... Yes!
Then he cannot be God. If Jesus is God, the answer must be yes to both or no to both; the separation of the two proves the difference.
Also he is referred to as the man Christ Jesus.
Is it not foolish talk that God should mediate for man by making plea's to himself?

It is amazing how these demonic pastors can cause you to dismiss simple common sense with their devil inspired philosophies.

EG: The temptations of Jesus.
Since God cannot be tempted, Jesus cannot be God.
At Luke 4:9-11
Satan uses Psalm 91:11-12 in an attempt to corrupt Jesus.
"God will give his Angels charge.... To keep you from harm"!
(Does he wish to corrupt God?)
Common sense people... If Jesus is God (As you claim) then he is the spirit behind the words of the psalm. (He spoke them)
How then can Satan attempt to make Jesus put a different spin on this psalm if they are Jesus' own words?
We know what we mean when we speak, even if it is wrong, yet we know what we mean.
Satan can only attempt to twist the meaning because he knows these are not Jesus' words but God's. In any case how can God be hurt by a fall or need the help of Angels?
Jesus had to refer to the words of God as do you and I when we answer: thus Jesus answers "it is said" or "It is written" though shall not temp the lord thy God.

Note once again Jesus is referring to what is written and not making himself the authority of the written word. Not to overlook that it has already been mentioned, God cannot be tempted.

Next we behold a stupendous error on the part of foolish Trinitarian reasoning.
Satan asks Jesus to worship him. Luke 4:7
You insult all that is common sense if you need an explanation of this.
I tell you truly; if you cannot see past your foolish reasoning at this point, all explanation will die on you.
God to worship the devil... Are you mad... Have you lost touch with all your senses... can you be this insane to believe that Satan would ask God to worship him?
I am actually in pain trying to remove this foolishness from you!

But Satan also adds;
"All this power/authority I will give you"
How is it possible for you to be this blind?
Frankly I'm becoming tired of these childish antics; having to prove and explain to you how this is impossible.
That God could want anything that Satan has; (even we want nothing from him) and to imply that Satan hold's power over God by offering to God what is his.
Note also Satan says it was given to me. Demonic pastors say Adam gave it to Satan, and so you are lost.
However, God says different.
Daniel 4:17// Deuteronomy 10:14.
Read it!!!

Why do you allow these demonic pastors to so quickly overturn your common sense?

But know this... you shall bear the guilt along with them; for they could not do this to you were you not already that way inclined.
They only needed to feed your wicked spirit by using texts that can be twisted.
IE: Acts 20:28// John 1:1 and you become stupefied.
It did not work on Jesus, but will work on the hypocrite.

Now I beg you... please stop this madness!
I find your obstinacy most confusing! Is this type of behaviour not proof that you are being deceived? How your arrogance and self conceit still remains is amazing.
But like your father the devil you are relentless.

How is it you do not stumble over these words; which are written:
"No man has seen God at any time",
but you continue to declare Jesus to be God whom man have seen?

Tell me which of these things presents you with the problem; is it Jesus, God or the bible? For you keep contradicting them all; throwing his words behind you, replacing God's written words with your own emotional sentiments!
If Jesus is God as these hypocrites or these demonised preachers profess, then God lied to Moses when he said:
Exodus 33:20.
"No man may see God and yet live"!

Did man not see Jesus?
It is also written: "it is impossible for God to lie"
Hebrews 6:18.
For my part I accept that the one who is the liar is the devil. And are you still confused or are you content to knowingly be a devil worshiper, persecuting God and playing at righteousness? Repent of this offence! Repent!!! Offer your prayer of apology. Throw away your pride and say to God:
I am sorry; I am in error; I was mislead!

Behold... Hebrews 9:24 Jesus goes into heaven itself to make an appearance in the presence of God. Well then, did he go into heaven to meet himself?
Hypocrites, offspring of vipers, sons of the devil; Will you not quit twisting scripture?

And so you by-pass obvious scriptures to create your own demon inspired theology.
"For God so love the world that he gave his only begotten son"....
Who is it that does not know this scripture? What don't you understand? If he is begotten then he had a beginning, if a son then there is also a father, and also a beginning, (What human being does not know this?) the truth is in your face... it is in your face... It is in the word "son". What son has no beginning? Son is the by-product of another. So then neither in being a son or being begotten can he be God. He told you these words himself in many places but you cannot hear because you are not his kind.

When did you take on the mantle of the Devil? Were you blind sided without noticing? For you make

yourself a rebel of the word; you've become an adversary of God? Can you repent of this or is there already too much dead flesh; too much wickedness?
Satan is able to trip you because you neglect words God himself says in favour of your insight or words from someone you respect above God; your peers or your pastors, who themselves are often servants of demons. You go beyond the written word to establish your intellect. This is the reason why you are confused.

The devil contradicts God; Eve was seduced by that which contradicts Gods word! She should not have concluded something different to that which she knew God had spoken. Adam contradicted God as you now also do.

*It is **impossible** to say Jesus is God's son and be wrong...*
For this fact is known to all...
God spoke it and it is written.
But when you say Jesus is God you risk blasphemy.
Why not be content with what you are sure of?
You cannot find one single scripture (And the bible is a big book) where Jesus makes claims to anyone that he is the true God. (Watch out for the subtleties of demon pastors and their reasoning on what Jesus did, for Jesus himself says this proves I'm who I say I am). Again I make it clear that I am aware that Jesus bears the title of God; a title also placed on many others on various occasions, even the devil) But since there is only one true God you are either being deceived or are your selves' devils and deceivers in opposition to God!
But for sure with this false hood you will not see life.

The deeper you dig your hole; the harder it will be for you to climb out!

Out of the mouth of Jesus himself comes these words:......

John 17:3 "This is eternal life that they may know You... the only true God ... and Jesus Christ whom you have sent"

Jesus says the father in heaven is **the only true God; and he Jesus is the one the father has sent.**
Why do you contradict him, do you wish to deny this also; Is it God or the devil you fight?

John 8:25 "I am the one I have always claimed to be". *(What is his claim)?*
John 14:6 "I am the way, the truth and the life *(But God is your destination)* no one come to the father except through me"

Now you devils with your demon inspired teachings; will you please stop your nonsense; and go back into your pit! (Does the cap fit; is it the one you are wearing?)

These pastors, (Either blind or simply hypocrites) all of them, agents of the devil! Teachers with fat bellies! Playing you like a drum; confirming the empty vessels you are, it is yet possible to escape.
Flee whilst you can, it will get harder later.

Once you are capture you are then shaped into use for the deception and destruction of others.
(Yep; a witch or a bitch for Satan)

But their hypocrisy runs deeper.
They always run to John 1:1 to seek refuge to find shelter for their beliefs.
It matters not that the passage speaks of one being with another, which implies two beings, not three; as there is no Holy spirit here (A scripture from the beginning without a Trinity) but you are stretched to conclude it is one and the same person.(Simply different manifestations of God). Should one feel sorry for you; surely this is now what you deserve for allowing yourself to be abused and confused by childish arithmetic's?

John 1:14. Then the one being the word becomes flesh; leaves the other behind and comes to earth. Though you read it,
(Yet you do not listen) that this one is the begotten son of the father who left his position.
It is written "we beheld his glory, the glory of the only begotten of the father". Will the demon in you not relent; will you not concede? Must you contend this also?

But again, the absolutely unassailable point, almost impossible to contradict; and cannot be deflected; **(Which again needs your attention)** *is where it says:*
John 1:18
"No man has seen God at any time"
the only begotten son, which is in the bosom of the father, he hath declared him.

If the only begotten son resting in the bosom of the father refers to Jesus whom we have seen, can he be God? And who is the God in whose bosom he rests,... that no man has seen; Please explain; if no man has seen God, who is Jesus?

Hypocrites; you sons of the devil; enemies of the living God and of everything righteous; will you ever relent, are you no longer able to quit?

Acts 13:10

O man, full of every sort of fraud and villainy, you son of the devil; you enemy of everything righteous, will you not quit distorting the way of the LORD?...

It therefore follows that like him you are blinded for a time.

When the devil is trapped in his lies he then looks for a better opportunity, or as it is written; another convenient time.

Are you a devil? Your day will have its end soon enough! You cannot claim innocents when your conscience is corrupt and you seek to preserve it at all cost from being exposed.
You work for Satan the devil.
For only a devil will keep contending these things?

Above it has been shown where Jesus said:
John 8:43-44 "Why is my language not clear to you, why can you not understand what I'm saying? (You cannot hear my words) Because you are from your father the Devil and you wish to carry out his desires"!

So then although you may find this offensive, remember, these are not my words.

*You cannot have the spirit of God and declare Jesus to be God. Jesus calls God father; why do you contradict him, why not accept what he says and do as he does?
But noooo...! You contend even with Jesus; guess you already know your god is the devil.*

John 11:22/27 *"I know that even now. That as many things as you ask God for; God will give you..... I have believed that you are the son of God"*
To which God does Martha refer, what is her belief?

John 4:24-26 When speaking to the Samaritan woman Jesus identifies God as a spirit and confirms himself to be the messiah (The anointed one) with the words; I am he!

John 9:35-37 (I am the son of man)
Can God be a son of Man? What madness possesses you people... as if I didn't already know! What better opportunities can there be for him to say he is God?

John 11:41-42 *"Father I thank you that you have heard me"!* (Is that not self explanatory)?
To whom does Jesus speak? Is he mad or are you... you who are trying to confuse me with your foolishness?

"I said these things for the benefit of the people standing here"
Yet it does not benefit you... why?
For your benefit he spoke those words. If you gained no

benefit, well then, it was not for you. You cannot claim to be his follower.

John 14:28 "I am going to the father, for the father is greater than I".
Does this not imply two separate beings, a father and a son? Is Jesus simply making this all up; confusing us on purpose. Does he claim to be God or to be as great as God, or is it you who are making a mockery of the scriptures looking for loopholes to inject poison?

Luke 10:21-22

"I …publicly… praise you father lord of heaven and earth….you have hidden these things…. All things have been committed to me by my father….no one knows who the father is"!

Jesus makes it public (This is for all to hear and to know) that he is not God. Are you still unable to hear him? Does your question still remain?
In the abundance of water the fool is thirsty, and so I continue.

Isaiah 9:6
Though it calls him mighty God it states also that he is a prince, a position God cannot hold. God is not simply mighty, but ALMIGHTY and second to no-one.
Though it says he is the everlasting father, yet this only makes him a second Adam. (Incidentally Adam is also called son of God) He is now the replacement of Adam as our father, but not the replacement of almighty God as father. These things you are also told. (Jesus also taught you this in prayer) If you cannot hear him you are not his sheep! If your spirit were free you would know these things are

true and not try to contradict what is obvious with things you say are mysteries.

Your confusion is your own doing. You, the one wishing to honour men, will respond to the irritation of your spirit by seeking out your pastor for help in justifying your false belief; to help you justify your stance, and they will; for he/she is complicit in this evil, either in ignorance or by design.
But do not overlook the fact that scripture also call Satan god... by holy authority therefore...,
Satan the devil is also a mighty god.

From Romans to Revelation; every book Paul and others write, they open in the first three verses with the explanation that they are slaves both to God and of Jesus.
They separate God from Jesus in person.
Read them; what do you see? Yet such overwhelming evidence is no use to you, I wonder why?
Though the real God was pointed out to pharaoh, he refused to change his stance. He was not innocent, he asked Moses to pray to God to remove these frogs; why not ask his magicians, whom he believes serves the gods? That will be true of many of you as you seek solutions... for....

it is not the real God you seek.
You seek only an excuse to continue your foolish behaviour; hoping that someone else helps you shoulder the blame.

Yet did God not tell me this in the beginning?

However, there are other so-called educated ones who claim that since Jesus says:
John 8:58 before Abraham was "I AM"; and that this proves him to be God by virtue of the fact that he uses the same title by which God refers to himself at Exodus 3:14.

Really...!.!.!.!?????
This is so ridiculous it is beyond funny.

What simplistic nonsense! Should these wizards/sorcerers with their trickery be taken seriously? Will you throw all other proven points in the toilet to substantiate this foolishness? It is hard to contain my laughter, my sadness and my anger at the foolishness of you people, yet I try to contain myself so as not to stumble you; in case you also believe them.

It is either total blindness; a reach of extremmmme stupidity; a deliberate sin ridden conscience or satanic possession that causes anyone to claim Jesus to be God based on this saying. Sheer nonsensical and idiotic desperation to promote a lie!
Hypocrites; blind Pharisee's!

Unravel this: Jesus says with God all things are possible; yet Paul says it is impossible for God to lie. (Which is correct?) Since one appears to contradict the other surely they cannot both be correct? (But they are).
Why then would you now attempt to justify this? Because you know things are not as simplistic as they appear.. there in lies the lesson.

Samuel said to God: Here I AM!
Isaiah said to God: Here I AM!
And on many other different occasions in sentence construction it is also said.
Paul said, become imitators of Christ even as I AM!
Even the healed blind man said: I AM he!
Do you make these ones God also merely by the contraction of a noun, or the mere mention of the term I AM?

You are having a laugh...!!! Should such false preachers not be rebuked? Also you too should be ashamed that with such little guile and such little subterfuge the devil is able to disarm you and turn you?
You people are feeding on ashes!

As mentioned previously, the bible is a big book, why do you think God would be so elusive in revealing himself when at the same time wanting to be known by the world?
He told you: Isaiah 43:10-11 "I have chosen you to know and to believe there is no other God, there never was and never will be"! Was that Jesus speaking? Of course not!

Mark 12:29-30 The lord our God is the one lord...
This is Jesus who is speaking is it not?
Is he referring to himself?

Mark 12:36 The LORD said to my lord sit at my right hand. We know Jesus sits at the right hand of God, who then is the God besides whom he sits? Who speaks to whom?
What ignorance possesses you?
As if I do not already know!
King James Bible explains in its preface: When the word LORD is written in capital letters it refers to Jehovah.

....

On occasion Jesus marvelled, (by implication he was surprised) Mark 6:6 // Mathew 8:10
Can anyone catch God by surprise?

....

Jesus on occasion said "I do not know"!
I do not know is ignorance of a fact. Can God say this; is there anything to which God is ignorant?

....

Oh you blind, stubborn and senselessly wicked people; what will it take to convince you; for what reasons do you continually reject God and common sense?

Matthew 4:9
How then can you be this easily beguiled...can the devil give God anything;... how can Jesus be God?
To ask God to "fall down" and show an act of submission!
Not only would he be a madman; but now so are you. I'm sorry but my senses are screaming as to how anyone can be this blind.

Take as another example:
Luke 8:28-30
A man infested with demons.
The demons plead: Jesus, son of the most high God; I beg you, do not torment me.
(First we acknowledge that the demon says Jesus is the son of the most high God). Do you concur?
He had been ordering the unclean spirit to come out of the man.
(Second we acknowledge that the demons do not immediate comply... can any demon out rightly refuse God in this manner?)

Thirdly Jesus asked: what is your name?
(Again this would imply he did not know, neither was he aware of the authority of this demon in charge; in that there were many.
The demons spoke as one man... I beg you.. never we beg you! Jesus must ascertain who or what is in control in this man). The leader demon then said: Legion, (Implied...I speak for all) because they are many of us. Therefore neither did Jesus have prior knowledge of its name or the status of these demons.

Do you mean to tell me o foolish man that these details can be hidden from God?

Perhaps you remember these words already spoken.
In the abundance of water only a fool is thirsty!
How can you claim ignorance in the face of all this abundance?
Surely you are being taught by demons and by now you must know it!

Hebrews 5:7-10
Jesus pleads with loud outcry (Screaming in emotional agony) and tears. (God crying, don't you get it?)
Must I explain why some one would cry tears?
(Your god cries tears...To whom?)
And he was heard;
by whom?
Jesus learned obedience by suffering.

Really!!???
You still do not accept it?
Does God need to learn anything, especially obedience... who then does he obey; who is his teacher!!? To whom does God become obedient?

This is Madness of the highest order;
yep...yep.. yep.
You know the devil is mad, and so are you; you cannot beg off being a madman if you choose to remain this stubborn. I tell you this defence becomes more exhausting by the minute... but you still remain stubborn, stiff-necked and rebellious!

Does God make himself suffer to teach himself how to obey, as though it is something he does not know or as

being responsible to someone else? Does God need to learn anything; does he need to attend your school?
What useless god are you talking about?

Was GOD called by GOD to be a priest also?
(I can hardly bring myself to ask such foolish questions)

Perhaps you will say he suffers to teach us, but for whom is he a priest; before whom does he officiate? Surely your senses are being offended by the inference of God being called by God to be a God whilst at the same time he himself is God.
Madness I tell you!!!

Jesus in the garden of Gethsemane was imploring God for help....
"take this cup away from me", or... I do not want to do this, is implied!
Whom ever it was he was talking to, they were not in agreement with each other!

Matt 27:46 "Eli Eli, Lama Sabachthani"!?
"My God, my God, why have you forsaken me"?
(From God's mouth to whose ears)

There are those who will quote Thomas' words; "my lord and my God", but will ignore Jesus' words.

If you receive witness from men, should not the witness from God be greater; he who testifies concerning his son?

Only by now using arguments orchestrated by the devil and his progeny will you be able to construct a contradictory response to circumvent the common sense reasoning and scriptural information here provided.

CHAPTER 7

JESUS CONFESSES HIS ORIGIN

I've heard of a donkey that talked ... even a serpent that walked...and dead bones that came to life....but I'd be a monkey's uncle if they con me into believing that God can die....! Yes... I'd be done believing in anything if I can be conned into believing this lie.

Jesus explains his purpose!
For this I was born and came into the world …as a witness of truth! (Yet put to death!)

Is God not immortal? Immortality cannot die! How then is Jesus to be God and yet not fit this criteria;… he died did he not? (Put out of existence)
Only the most severe hypocrite requires proof of this!

John 6:57 ## "I live because of the father"
If Jesus is God there should be no harm in the father saying I live because of Jesus. But Jesus being the son was brought into existence by his father who is the real God.

Revelation 3:14 ## "…the beginning of the creation of God".
Here Jesus speaks of his origin. God created me; brought me into being.

John 20:17/21 How do you read?
"I ascend to my father, and to your father; to my God and to your God"
By implication Jesus says that God is the same to me as he is to you. My father and yours, my God and yours!

Let us imagine for an instant that this explanation is flawed (though Jesus himself spoke the words)… from what type of heart does your contradiction come, and what other explanation can you give better than that of Jesus; that does not issues from a wicked and deceptive heart?

"As the father sent me, even so I send you".

Hebrews 1:8-9
"Your throne o God (Jesus) is for ever and ever… therefore God (Jehovah) your God has anointed you…."

Please help me somebody; if this tells you that Jesus is almighty God, then I confess I'm totally blind.

John 16:26-28
My blindness is eating me alive… Please help me God! How does everyone see and yet I cannot?

Jesus bears the title God as he is born of God. (It is written: Gods only begotten son)

This you know: A donkey gives birth to a donkey as a cat gives birth to a cat. So too, God gives birth to God. Whatever monster you may birth spiritually, I know physically you give birth only to a human.

John 17:3 This scripture is extremely potent; it cannot be deflected and so it should constantly be in your face and referred to:
"Now this is eternal life; that they may know you, the only true God and Jesus Christ whom you sent"!

Jesus is here speaking. If you need me to again explain this verse then you are truly lost and far outside God's grace.

A note worthy point that I believe is often overlooked. As flesh is born of flesh, spirit is born of spirit. But Jesus

*was born of spirit before and after his flesh.
Note; Jesus (whom you say is God) had a birth.*

*Hebrews 1:5-6 "Today you have become my son"!
Since he was and is spirit, yet "today" (this day) you
have become my son, who is it that speaks; and whatever
interpretation you may bring to the table, first understand
it speaks of a birth, a beginning to a relationship.
God's spirit gave birth to him! (Yes or no)?
Do you still conclude he give birth to himself?
Yet God is not born of anything... he just is!*

*ICorinthians 15:24-28
The father has delivered all things into his son's hands.
This is a temporary arrangement as all things must return
to the father, and Jesus must subject himself to God His
father so that God is God over all.*

*Again I ask you; did Jesus at anytime say he is God?
Yet there were many opportunities to do so.
Even the statement "I and the father are one" does not
make this a revelation that he is God. For he explained "I do
nothing of my own initiative, but only what the father tells
me".
Which statement simply means we are in agreement!*

*John 8:25
The crowds and Pharisees demanded.
Who are you? Jesus responded, "The one I have been
claiming to be from the beginning"!*

*He had just told them where he is from.
Yet those rebellious and hypocritical Pharisees rejected*

all he said, looking for convenient words whereby they may have him killed.

John 8:53... They ask again:
Who is it that you are making yourself out to be?
Jesus answered: *"I do not glorify myself.... it is my father* who you say is your God *who glorifies me, and yet it is clear you do not know him"!*
Well then do you know him?

John 7:29//8:29... *I know him... that one sent me and will not abandon me because I always do that which is pleasing to him.* Jesus says he knows God..!!!???
Wow!!! So why are you still blind?

Consider carefully John 8:24
If you do not believe that I am he (God's son)
you will die in your sin.
You who say he is someone other than who he claims to be, are you not also sinning, will you not also die in your sin?
And yet as you also do, they kept on asking:
John 10:24-26.... How long will you keep our souls in suspense; if you are the Christ tell us plainly?

Jesus said *"I told you already but you did not listen"!* (This is the frustration I have with you)
What is it he kept saying that they were unable to hear, and unwilling to accept?
He kept saying "I... am... God's... son"!
John 10:36 "I said.... I am God's son"

Are you also deaf, unwilling or demonised?

Now consider the moments before he died?

"Father, take this cup away from me… yet not as I will but as you will"!

Is God's will and Jesus Christ's will the same?

Here Jesus is in opposition to this course, so whose will is it that must be obeyed?

On the cross:

"Father forgive them, they know not what they do"!

Why does Jesus make such a nonsense statement if he is God? Why defer to some other God?
Why not forgive them himself,
Should he not simply say I forgive you?
(As he earlier did)?

Still on the cross:

Eli, Eli lama sabachtani!

Words you seek to bend to your own destruction.

My God, My God why have you forsaken me?

Still on the cross:
Final moment before entering into 3days of non-existence:

"Father into your hands I commit my spirit"!

Surely now you are suggesting that Jesus has a mental problem or is schizophrenic.
Does he of sound mind commit himself to himself;
or will you accept Satan has been lying to you?

How many times are you to see Jesus debating with his

father and yet you will not believe?

How many times does the father say no to Jesus and yet you will not accept?
They are not the same person!

Who hardened you this way? What will it take for you to recover?
Is it your intention to make fools of us all by persuading us that Jesus was a madman, talking to him self?

He said: if you do not believe I am he "You will die in your sins"! If you will not believe anything
Believe this! You will die in your sins!

I find it to be an impossible thing that anyone could read through the book of John and at its conclusion say that Jesus is God.
It is not possible to be this blind unless it is supernatural.

However if one includes deliberate ignorance or a devilish agenda then the impossible being held up by lies is possible to the fool. You are simply being told what you want to hear.

Let us see why this is:
Every chapter in the book of John is a revelation of Jesus Christ.
One wonders; how can such things be circumvented with such regularity.

2Corinthians 4:3-4
Where it is written.. If our Gospel is veiled (Hidden) it is veiled only to those who are perishing, in their case the god

of this world (devil) has blinded the mind of the unbelievers to keep them from seeing the light of the gospel of the glory of Christ who is the likeness (Image) of God and that it may not shine upon them.

Does this Book not say the devil has hypnotized the entire planet?

All mankind are blinded for damnation!
If you do not have a death wish, then try to escape!

Jesus says: I am your brother.
God is not my brother, but my God, **he is God to all including Jesus.**
Simple conclusion.. God cannot die and yet Jesus did.......!

No matter how much you insist on dancing with the devil; no matter how you dance this dance; or seek to bend scripture, there is no escaping this fact.

Jesus is not God almighty!

CHAPTER 8

GOD IS NOT A TRINITY!

Who then is he?
Well I've seen a dragon –fly ...and I've seen a house –fly ...I even know a fool who thought he could fly... but I'd be done believing anything... now I'm done believing this lie..!

The Egyptian and Babylonian trinity were here long before Jesus Christ. Why are Christians now taking lessons from demons?
Did the Egyptians and Babylonians have true worship; why then are your beliefs the same?

*They believed the Trinity long before you did!
Imagine this triune being like the 3 angles on a triangle;
now imagine the 3 angles like that on a pyramid, you know
the one. If you can use your imagination I need not explain
further... you know this is the Devil.*

*Incidentally; arguments thus far has already dismissed the
thought of there being a third living and equally powerful
being called the Holy Spirit, as another great lie!*

A lie can only be defended with another!

*This lie is what they call the trinity and they proclaim it as
a mystery.
Ha ha ha..! Foolish people!
(Of course it's a mystery, and you are blind).
Why is it a mystery... because it simply cannot be defended
or clearly explained! It is a lie!
But how deep does the rabbit hole go?*

*There is a **Hindu trinity**: Vishnu/Bhrama/Sheva!*
Do you accept these as God?
*There is a **Babylonian trinity**: Isis /Nimrod /Tammuz.*
Biblical rejects!
*The **Egyptian trinity** is ... Osiris/horus/isis*
More devilish stuff!
*There is also the **Satanic trinity**: Dragon/Wild beast/False
prophet.*
Truly Satanic!
Then there is your trinity.. Father, son, and Holy Spirit!
**All sorcery and witchcraft; tools in the hands of the devil!
All these beliefs are manipulated by a master!**

But when the devil finally meets up with you; he will have to put his tail between his legs and run; for the magnitude of evil from some of you makes him look childish and innocent by comparison.

*The trinity is explained as God in three persons.
In other words Jesus; the Holy Sprit and the father are all the same person. He (God) is merely showing himself in different ways; they are equal because they are the same...
All lies! Have you been asleep all this time?*

*The first cut is deep; and now herein lies the pain in all the lies that must be undone.
(Can you untie the knot?)*

*Anything can be made to appear as a trinity.
Luke 23:46*

"Father into your hands I commit my spirit"!
*(You now have the father, son and the spirit all together)
But do you care to know o empty man, that three parties being mentioned together does not constitute a trinity?
(You are clutching at straws).
Never has common sense up and deserted another this quickly; nor have I seen reasoning this badly impaired!
That anyone could be this blind..!*

*A) Jesus at one point died, which leaves two; where now is the trinity? Can God die?
B) Jesus offers up his spirit; did the Holy Spirit also die with him?
C) Jesus commits all to the father; (Then there was one) he being the only one left alive.
This must stop! "You will die in your sin"!*

(These hypocrites are now pushing the boundary another step further, making additional implications in defence of this foolishness, which incidentally works only on the Godless)

The others pagan beliefs do not necessarily claim that their gods are equal or that they are 3 in 1.
It is also noteworthy that they had their beliefs before yours. (All devils) Who then is copying whom?

Jesus here confirms that the trinity is a doctrine of the devil.
John 4:22-24
"You people worship what you do not know (And this you admit) but we worship what we know"!
Thus in one sentence ... if nothing more was written; Jesus here states salvation is not found in ignorance... you cannot be this ignorant of God and claim to know him.
Salvation is not found in ignorance.. We worship what we know; you worship a word not of God and one you cannot explain; a triune mystery and claim it to be God though you cannot explain it.

No one on this planet can correctly explain the trinity; the ignorance is obvious; hence they conclude it to be a mystery...
No; no; no...
It is not a mystery; it is a huge gargantuan lie of the devil. Did you not know the devil' a liar? Ok, you say it, but you don't believe or acknowledge it!
For you simply dance with the Devil in your attempt to dance around the scriptures.
God is worshipped in spirit and truth.

*All such Trinitarian hypocrites are liars!!!
Without truth, is what makes you delusional, therefore all that remains is for you to surrender to a mystery!*

*Is it that you cannot see, or that you will not?
Your blindness has purpose.*

2Corinthians 4:3-4.
You maintained your right to believe what you feel like, whether God approves or not. Satan also has a legal right to blind the minds of those who are his own.

Research the Nicene Creed of 325AD and you will learn the trinity was not instituted by God.

*Seems you people have something in common with the devil after all.
(Hello daddy)!*

*If you would only stop trying to prove how intelligent you are you would realise you speak words that are unrecognizable to God.
In short you are lying!*

You admit the word trinity is not in the bible.
*Big deal! Here you admit a truth, but it is only subterfuge; for next you camouflage it to promote the devil... you think to blind side people. Your superior wisdom has coined the word that makes you feel intelligent, and now you seek to make God's word defend it. Woe to you!
How can you engage in a war and call it God's war whilst at the same time spiritually murder people; for you admit, God did not actually say it? Then who said it? You and your father!*

Wake up!
I confront the devil in you! What will it take to unmask him?

It is written: Romans 3:4 "Let God be found true though every man be found a liar". [Here is why]... That you may be proved righteous in your words and might win when being judged!
You will be judged by your words!
When therefore God asks you where did you get your words of conviction, show me where I said those things? How do you expect to win when you cannot actually locate in scripture where he said it? Do you think it will suffice for you to say to God ...when you said father, son, and Holy Spirit; I thought this was what you were trying to say?
Fool.......! do you not fear God at all?
Oh how I pity you, for you are dead man walking!

Matt 28:18-19
"....... go baptise in the name of the father, son and Holy Spirit"!
Does this prove a trinity? It does not!

I repeat; three names being mentioned together does not give validity or divine right for a trinity; neither is it evidence of equality.
Father, Mother and Child can be mentioned in one breath; but there is no equality here implied.

Why then should Father, Son and Holy Spirit?

Jehovah is the father. Jesus is the son. The Holy Spirit is the Holy Spirit...
Does he have another name?
Do you even care?

*By now you should know that the Holy Spirit is not a ghost.
God is spirit, have you not been told?
At the preface of my King James bible version;
(Yes that is what it is; a version) it says:
"The king James version uses the word ghost for spirit".
Who gave them this right to make these insertions?
Surely you are aware that it is written; John 4:24 "God is spirit" again the king James stumble, for it says "God is a spirit" thus even in this tampering there are contradicting words; too numerous to show at this juncture. But here is the big one and the results that befall all who will not tell it like it is.*

*That this is overlooked is incredible:
1John 5:7 in the King James Version (Bible) this is a diabolical insertion; a monstrous attempt at deception......*

"For there are three that bear record in heaven; the Father, the Word, and the Holy Ghost; and these three are one...."

*Even was that insertion authentic
(and other bibles deny that it is)
Yet it cannot disprove Jesus to be God's son.*

An explanation on the Holy Spirit will follow.

*The three being one is the same as all his children being one.
John 17:21-23 Merely an expression of unity and agreement!*

This is a dastardly attempt to provoke a doctrine of the trinity!

1John 5:8 says there are three that bear witness in earth; the Spirit; and the water; and the blood and the three agree in one.
No living persons or living thing here to provoke a trinity. Merely inanimate things that proves how God has provided a witness for us in his son!

If we receive the witness men give; the witness God gives is greater. Which witness do you invoke?

To find another translation, even another version with these extended words of three witnesses in heaven and that these three are one, takes some doing.
Why are these words absent from so many other bibles?
You decide!
They tamper with bibles in an attempt to deceive.

To illustrate; the Holy Bible... Revised Standard Version... deletes the suffering of Jesus Christ.

Luke 22:43-44 Why?
His plea's (God help me) and an appeal to God in a situation of undeniable weakness, even in expressing fear of what must now come to pass would prove to all this is not God. It is also undeniable evidence which proves he did not have the mind of God as they were not in agreement with each other.

God; by his refusal to co-operate with Jesus shows they were not of the same will. Thus Jesus says "let your will (Not mine) be done"!

Other New bible versions are now making other changes: and yet others simply make deletions.

"All authority has been given me"!
Does God need authorization from anyone?
Who then gave Jesus (Your God) this authority?

He (God) has testified of his son! These false preachers give you testimony of another God.

He lets them fail in their prophecies and fall on their faces, but you go and pick them back up.

Oh you sad people; glutton for punishment; what next must he prove to you?
2Corinthians 13:14
Again I say, if you are trying to make a connection here, it is merely to console your ego.
(This is your pink elephant)
This point has been thoroughly established.
The grace of Jesus; the love of God, and the fellowship of the Holy Spirit are the necessary condiments of all Gods children.
(Proof of God's approval)
Jesus is the way to God. (Not God himself)
Holy Spirit is the helper; fellowship of God himself.
(The connection to God bearing his essence, identity, character and power; it is what he is).
And God is God, our heavenly father. Who bears his essence and is therefore called spirit.
I beg you, end this madness please!!!
Please, please, please stop this insanity; you merely hasten your doom, for this is a certainty...
You will die in your sins!

Luke 11:45
By saying these things you offend us also……. If you are offended also… woe unto you!

If then you cannot think in spirit, how can you know God who is understood only by spirit?

1Corinthians 2:10-14

God has revealed it by his spirit, for the spirit searches all things even the deep things of God.... No one knows the things of God except by his spirit…Not words taught by human wisdom, but words that are of God… The man without spirit cannot accept these things… they are foolishness to him, he cannot get to know them because they are examined spiritually.

So then we ought not to be too surprised by the failures of those not in God's intimate group.

CHAPTER 9

HOLY SPIRIT GOD DECEPTION!

Now here is one for your dairy; these hypocrites claim the Holy ghost had Sex with Mary.... For if he is a person as they claim and a child was born in his name they have become God's judge and his jury.

*So what is the spirit of God?
Is it a person, a thing; an it; or a he?
Is it of God or is he another being with God.*

The Holy Spirit is God. (John 4:24) Who in actuality is the first spirit, the one and only; and not a third being which represents a trinity.

But you prefer to accept a triune mystery, something you know you cannot explain or defend because it is a lie from the pit of hell, (Pardon the expression) far too complex to explain without lies; so you become a devil. You are on your own for in this Satan cannot help you.

I see the devil confronting God; I see the devil tempting Jesus. Now you o empty man, can you reveal where he confronts or tempts the Holy Spirit?

Go baptise in the name of the father, son and Holy Spirit does not confer trinity; are you a child?

God is a Spirit person, (But not a spirit) an Angel is a spirit.

An Angel is not merely Spirit as God is not merely Spirit; but consciousness within energy.
Humans are consciousness within flesh.
The flesh is of no use whatsoever!

Holy Spirit is the complete essence of who God is, the character and embodiment of all that is God.

All Gods abilities combined into his character is called Holy Spirit.

As Solomon showed, even a cat has a spirit.

Now tell me (You who believe that holy spirit is part of a triune being) how is it that we can blaspheme Jesus Christ; even blaspheme the father; and it can all be forgiven ....
But blasphemy against the Holy Spirit can never be forgiven? How can this Spirit being you confer Godhood upon carry

more influence than even the father?
I don't want to have the burden of this foolishness so it is left for you to explain.
If you offend one do you not offend all?

Fools rush in where wise men fear to tread!

He has been trying to show you that the Holy Spirit cannot be a third God, carrying more honour and prestige than even the father and the son. But you are simply a stubborn and stiffed necked people.

Why do you offend him? What yet is he lacking in his effort to explain this? But I forgot you have no fear of God or death.

Father, into your hands I commit my spirit!
(Matthew/luke)
Or to paraphrase: I commit my life or life force, my essence, my existence, all that I am…
into your hands.

John 6:63 It is the spirit that gives life, the flesh is of no use whatsoever.
The life of the flesh is in the blood.
The life of the blood is in the spirit.
The life of the Spirit is in God.

(And so, the blood of Abel called to God)

John 3:6
What has been born from flesh is flesh, and what has been born from Spirit is Spirit.
The Spirit is the life; the flesh is of no use!

John 8:44... You are from your father the devil, and you wish to do the desires of your father....
How is the spirit of the devil in these people?
Is it not by their behaviour which bears a similarity to the devil?
All Adam's offspring are of the devil. This is by a spirit force implanted within; we are born in sin; born outside God with a rebellious spirit in us; and this is where the name of the devil was derived; he stands for rebellion. This does not imply actually possession at birth. But we must be born again of a different spirit and in favour with God. Yes! All mankind are born devils; and we stay devils until we are born again In Jesus.

John 4:24
God's spirit... is God. Not a separate being. Give ear to this saying also: Since it says God must be worshipped in spirit and truth; if one is not truthful, one cannot have the spirit. The spirit is not given to those who cannot accept truth. Liars have no place in God's Presence.

His spirit is the essence of himself, or his character. (I am that I am) He is what he is! (Unquantifiable)

If you are Abraham's offspring then do the works of Abraham. (Be of the same spirit or show the same character)

TRY TO EXPLAIN THIS!
The exact same scenario in the story told by Mathew and Luke which defines what the Holy Spirit is.

Matthew 12:28....I cast out devils by the Spirit of God!
Luke 11:20.... I cast out devils by the finger of God!

Here the Holy Spirit is being explained; it is the same or identical scriptural passage and occasion, only with the obvious difference in its expression;
(Namely that Gods Spirit and Gods finger are one and the same thing) if you are still determined to remain rebellious stubborn, and untruthful, what is it that you are now promoting; you prove only your wickedness.

Once more we read: 2Corinthians 3:3
...... "Written not with ink but with the spirit of the living God"
And now the comparison: Exodus 31:18
..... "Written with the finger of God"
(Again his finger is in comparison with his spirit)

Acts 7:51-58
You rebellious and stiff-necked people, always resisting the Holy Spirit for self aggrandizement; will you also have me stoned? Well then, build up the sins of your forefathers and know as Jesus Christ lives, you are also his persecutor.

Ezekiel 37:6...put breath in you..
Ezekiel 37:14...put my spirit in you..
Same explanation to restore dead bones except the spirit is here now being replaced by breath.

Look again John 20:22
Jesus breathes and says Receive the Holy Spirit.
Acts 1:8: You will receive power when the Holy Spirit comes.
All one and the same spirit!

Genesis 1:2: The spirit of God moved upon the surface of the waters.
Gen 2:7: God blew breath (Spirit) into man.

Numbers 11:17: I will take OF the spirit that is upon you and place IT upon them!
How can God's spirit be called an it?
IT cannot be a person...; wake up people!

You devils.... Let my people go!

Cleanse your hearts; Save yourself; you are being dragged to the slaughter house. (By Judas goats)
How is it you cannot resist this Satanic foolishness?

ICorinthians 2:10-14
But God has revealed It to us by his spirit. The spirit searches all things, even the deep things of God. For who among men know the thoughts of a man except the man's spirit within him? In the same way no one knows the thoughts of God except the spirit of God.
We have not received the spirit of the world, but the spirit which is of God, that we may understand what God has freely given us. Which things also we speak, not in the words taught by human wisdom but in words taught by the spirit; expressing spiritual truth in spiritual words.

The man without the spirit does not accept the things that come from the spirit of God, for they are foolishness to him, because only those who have the spirit can understand what the spirit means.

The question now remains, as to whether these words are also foolishness to you or whether you are now beginning to understand.

God is not a limited body, but an unlimited spirit!

CHAPTER 10

THE PLEASURES OF AN ETERNAL LIFE

Truth is only veiled from the one who is perishing!
(So it is written)
Welcome home my children!

With all these negative words and all these hardships we face; what is the value of seeking or even serving God?
What is the point of it all?
Why not simply enjoy myself and accept my damnation?
Why should I care if I perish?
What can possibly be worth the hardships that I suffer daily for my beliefs or for Gods pleasure?
Indeed that option of rejecting God is open to all.
It is not compulsory to serve, but a choice.

(Recall Adam rejected it)

Yet if we are willing to face facts; whatever choice we make we suffer.
Do you suppose that the wicked have an easy time?
Was it easy when you were wicked, or is it easy now?

So then the choice is not concerning suffering; but how and for what we are willing to suffer.

Nearly all things (that I'm aware of) begins in hardship, even without God.
If I reject God I will still be in hardship, It Is Inescapable.

However, when the completion comes, will it be worth all the hardship I have endured, all this pain and this waiting?

Now comes the good part.
Perhaps too astonishing even to believe!

Here then is the promise of God and the completion of all our hardships.

Sealed with a kiss:

You are godlike, I have made you in my image; did I not tell it to you at the beginning?
How is possible for you to be made in my image, according to my likeness (Not leaving anything out) and still be less than a god? Jesus called you brothers for a reason!

On completion of the task you have been assigned, you will have proven your love, your likeness and your humility, along with your desire to obey. You shall be my child, an immortal god; you will be changed in the twinkling of an eye; any and everything you require or desire you shall be able to obtain.

(By your own will) You simply cannot be harmed or overthrown by anything; neither shall you know heartache, suffering or sorrow of any kind anymore forever.

You shall be changed to be literally a spirit being and not one of flesh.
(Flesh gives birth to flesh and spirit to spirit)
I have already told you these things.
Now please believe me!

The entire universe will be remade as your playground. You are no longer a goldfish in a bowl, but a godchild! And yes I have already told you these things.

If today you work and suffer to enjoy simple pleasures, was I asking too much of you for what I am offering? You are my child, and I am your father, because you have now accepted me!

Though a child may object to his schooling; in his later life he will understand the value in his education; as you now do.

You could not have been let loose on the universe without proper morals to guide you; and now that you have accepted them you are blessed forever.

Yes I knew there were those who required the reward without the work and will put to damnation anyone who tells them different, these were the weeds needing removal (gods onto themselves) they would eat any dish offered, though they knew it to be poisoned; rather than to endure any discomfort.

And so, now as you have proven yourselves it has been given all to you... you may do as you will; live in freedom and joy eternally for I have spoken!

*You are the reason behind all that has transpired; I was merely bringing you home.
It is the pure in heart that shall see God!*

May God and our Lord Jesus Christ be with you in all the empty places you must still walk!

*Written by: Mr Nobody!
Contact info :
mr.nobodyxxx777@gmail.com
kalix9@hotmail.com
(In case you still have questions)*

Conclusion

In conclusion I must say I begin to understand the suffering of our lord Jesus.

I spoke to you from the depths of my soul; so much so that I feel as though I was sweating blood.

However despite this they killed Jesus and I expect many of you will want to persecute me also.

I did not manufacture lies to corrupt your beliefs. There is no hidden agenda here.

But as the Pharisees said: (John 11:48) If we leave this man alone the Romans will take away our place and our nation.

Many of you cannot and will not repent, as your entire lives revolve around the place you're at or the position you hold.

If one sees the danger but will not speak he carries blood guilt. (Ezekiel 33:6-9//Acts 20:26-27)
This day I am clean of the blood of all you people in that I faithfully declared the word, and clearly showed the dangers.

I spoke to you truthfully, and now you in turn will act according to the spirit within you.

THE REAL GOD!

This is that you may know what is written within comes from an honest heart; respect for God and a desire for righteousness.

If you simply run with the crowd, you will not be enlightened, no matter what is spoken.

My hope is that the blessings within shall fall on you, and that you maybe amongst Gods chosen few.

www.ingramcontent.com/pod-product-compliance
Lightning Source LLC
Chambersburg PA
CBHW071505070526
44578CB00001B/442